# Teacher's Guide to
# COMPARISONS

## Reuven Feuerstein

IN COLLABORATION WITH

## Mildred B. Hoffman

**Teacher's Guide to Comparisons**

Authorized North American publisher and distributor:
SkyLight Professional Development
2626 S. Clearbrook Dr.
Arlington Heights, IL 60005
Phone 800-348-4474, 847-290-6600
Fax 847-290-6609
info@skylightedu.com
http://www.skylightedu.com

Creative Director: Robin Fogarty
Managing Editor: Julia E. Noblitt
Consulting Editor: Meir Ben-Hur
Editors: Sabine C. Vorkoeper, Amy Wolgemuth
Graphic Designer: Bruce Leckie
Cover and Illustration Designer: David Stockman
Instrument Artist: Eytan Vig
Type Compositor and Formatter: Donna Ramirez
Production Coordinator: Maggie Trinkle

© 1995 by R. Feuerstein, Hadassah–Wizo–Canada Research Institute, Jerusalem
All rights reserved.
Printed in the United States of America.

ISBN 0-932935-97-4

1543-CHG
Item number OTMS14

Z Y X W V U T S R Q P O N M L K J I H G F E D
06 05 04 03 02 01 00 99    15 14 13 12 11 10 9 8 7 6 5 4

# CONTENTS

| | |
|---|---:|
| **INTRODUCTION** | **1** |
| **UNIT I** | **11** |
| Cover Page | 16 |
| Page 1 | 22 |
| Page 2 | 29 |
| Page 3 | 33 |
| Page 4 | 40 |
| Pages 5–6 | 44 |
| **UNIT II** | **49** |
| Page 7 | 53 |
| Page 8 | 57 |
| Pages 9 and 11 | 62 |
| Page 10 | 69 |
| Pages 12–13 | 73 |
| **UNIT III** | **81** |
| Page 14 | 84 |
| Pages 15–16 | 88 |

# Teacher's Guide to Comparisons

# INTRODUCTION

## Objectives

To develop comparative behavior.

To increase and enrich the repertoire of attributes by which objects and events can be compared.

To introduce parameters for comparison that are characteristic, critical, and relevant to the needs that initiated the process of comparison.

To increase the ability to differentiate among parameters for comparison.

To make comparison a habit resulting in a spontaneous perception and description of the relationship between objects, events, and ideas in terms of their similarities and differences.

To provide concepts, labels, operations, and relationships with which to describe similarities and differences.

To develop those cognitive functions that are involved in comparative behavior at the input, elaboration, and output levels.

# I. CONCEPTUAL BASIS

## Need for Spontaneous Comparative Behavior

The ability to compare is basic to any cognitive process. Comparison not only is involved in recognizing and identifying the things we perceive, but is an essential prerequisite for establishing the relationships that lead to abstract thinking. It is through comparison that we organize and integrate separate and distinct bits of information into coordinated and meaningful systems of thought.

It is only when we spontaneously compare that we become modified by experience. As we receive new information, we organize, compare, and relate it to units of thought that already exist in our repertoire. We integrate this new information into these units of thought by finding the relationships between them. If a person does not attempt to organize and elaborate separate phenomena by seeking relationships between them through comparison, his or her experience will be limited to one of mere exposure to an episode.

## Mediation of Comparative Behavior

It is our intention to develop the comparative behavior of students. We will encourage their feeling of competency by increasing and enriching the repertoire of attributes to which experiences can be compared. We will provide students with concepts, labels, operations, and relationships to describe the similarities and differences among the stimuli they encounter. We will promote the students' feeling of independence and individuation by encouraging divergent responses and a flexibility in the use of parameters for comparison. We will mediate for control of behavior by discouraging impulsivity and encouraging responses that indicate reflection and differentiation among various parameters, and the selection of those that are most relevant.

## Lack of or Impaired Spontaneous Comparative Behavior

A lack of or impaired spontaneous comparative behavior results in an episodic grasp of reality in which things encountered are perceived as isolated, separate, one-time experiences. There is little or no effort to synthesize, to look for the relationships among the experiences of today and yesterday or tomorrow, or to put together two or more sources of information.

We are not implying that the person who does not compare spontaneously is incapable of doing so. It is rare that a child is unable to compare or does not do so spontaneously under special circumstances. Even a very young child will carefully select the larger of two pieces of candy offered to him or her. It may be, however, that for many people spontaneous comparison is limited to their most basic needs, which are not necessarily those that are relevant to academic achievement.

In other instances, when comparison is specifically requested, people may experience problems in responding because they lack the verbal tools needed to express their findings. Many of the differences between objects are either overlooked or not perceived because the concepts necessary for discrimination do not exist in one's repertoire or are not readily available. Additional difficulties may arise when the two objects under consideration are not compared using the same parameters. For example, it is true that a bird has feathers and a fish has gills, but this description is not a comparison. An adequate comparison requires that the fish and the bird be judged according to the same criterion: either skin covering (a fish has scales while a bird has feathers), means of respiration (a fish has gills while a bird has lungs), or any of the other many possibilities for identifying the similarities and differences between them.

## Nature of Comparison

Comparative behavior is a mental abbreviation of a motor process in which two elements are superimposed in order to find the points they share, and where and how they differ. Similarities and differences are then combined into a statement describing the relationship between the objects. The dimensions that are used are directly related to the needs and goals that generated the act of comparison in the first place.

Inducing comparison involves having an individual perceive and focus on two or more objects or events. To a large extent, when individuals are forced to compare, they must look for qualities they might otherwise not perceive. The act of comparison itself determines the nature of the perception—the sharpness of the elements that are perceived and the precision with which they are registered. Discrimination both stems from and determines the nature of comparison. Certain dimensions may be overlooked unless the object is compared with another that is different in those dimensions. In other words, an individual becomes aware of the relative characteristics of an object only when he or she compares it to another, since dimensions like "big" or "little" and "tall" or "short" cannot be perceived in a single object.

## Comparisons and Other Cognitive Functions

A number of cognitive functions are implicit in comparisons. Important are the following:

1. Clear, stable perception that is not to be changed in the course of comparison.

2. Conservation of constancies and invariants so that if an object of comparison is changed, continuity of that object is retained in spite of the changes that have occurred during the process of comparison. For example, if a word appears in large print at the top of a page and in small print at the bottom of a page, it should be recognized as the same word in spite of its change in size.

3. Systematic and thorough exploration that permits an exhaustive gathering of the data required for comparison. Without scanning the total field, the input of information will be poor, imprecise, and selected at random.

4. Precision in input and output that permits differentiation since unclear observations oversimplify and produce a global, nondiscriminating point of view.

5. Acquisition of labels, concepts, and operations since comparative behavior will depend on, as well as determine, the richness of the repertoire of the dimensions used in finding and describing similarities and differences. Refined discrimination is a function of having a great number of terms available to describe an object or phenomenon. While it might be easy to pick out a Siamese cat from among many different cats, it would be very difficult to find a specific blue coat on a rack of different coats without knowing exactly what it looked like. For instance, the following two requests would each have very different results: "Please get my blue coat. It is on the rack," versus, "Please get my coat. It is a long, blue, double-breasted coat with brass buttons. It is among the first four coats on the left side of the coat rack." The culture of an individual, his or her needs, and his or her familiarity with the object of comparison also affect the degree of similarity and difference that is perceived. For example, a trained botanist would perceive differences between two leaves that a layman would judge to be alike.

6. Summative behavior that sums and qualifies the dimensions by which elements are compared. We can place objects on a continuum ranging from totally different to identical simply by comparing the number of attributes they share with one another or with a representative model. Sometimes, however, the qualitative aspects outweigh the quantitative in forming a decision as to similarity-dissimilarity. A particular attribute may be so critical as to be more important than a great number of less essential characteristics. For example, we can compare two versions of an author's compiled works: one, a beautiful, hardbound volume, and the other a paperback version. While there are significant differences in the quantitative nature of the cost of these two volumes, the qualitative aspect is not affected by this attribute. The content of both is the same.

The process of judging, classifying, and establishing relationships is an important determinant for, as well as outcome of, comparative behavior.

## Invoked Comparison

Although we have stressed the need for spontaneous comparative behavior, invoked comparison, in which the student is specifically requested to compare, plays a major role in academic and vocational tasks and daily life. In fact, spontaneous comparison is a result of comparative behavior elicited by the environment at a very early stage of a child's development. The need to compare is both explicit and implicit in most school tasks. Even a question by a teacher, such as, "Is that the way to behave in class?," implies a need to compare norms of behavior.

Comparative behavior may, therefore, be the product of an intentional, volitional, and planned act on the part of the teacher or the student. In this instrument, we will try to teach students how to compare as a basis for their various cognitive activities and as a first step in making the comparative process both spontaneous and automatic. Once the need to compare becomes internalized and the process habitual, it is easy to move from comparing two perceived objects to comparing an object that is perceived to one that exists only in one's memory or imagination (or even to comparing two elements that are not present in the immediate perceptual field). Thus, by means of comparison and the relationships derived from the process, a person goes far beyond the perceptual aspects of the world and reaches a level of thinking that involves making inferences and judgments.

# II. OVERVIEW OF THE INSTRUMENT

## Enrichment of the Repertoire

Enrichment of the repertoire of concepts for comparison is both quantitative and qualitative. Quantitatively, the number of parameters should be greatly increased and flexibility in their use encouraged. For example, the students' usual response in comparing a city, a town, and a village is that the first is large, the second is medium sized, and the third is small. Brainstorming will reveal many other possible dimensions. These include population, area, highways, roads, lighting, sewage system, water supply, commerce, industry, employment opportunities, transportation, pollution, taxes, crime rate, parks, educational institutions, schools, libraries, sports and recreation areas, youth activities, health services, per capita income, and residents' longevity, health, mortality rate, birth rate, tooth decay, vocations, ethnic origin, and per capita spending.

Information should be gathered about each of the parameters and presented in a table or used as a basis for a profile of each setting. Findings should be compared for similarities and differences. The products of comparison can be used to answer questions and make value judgments on such issues as the quality of life, job opportunities, or pollution. An example is provided in table 1.

Whenever possible, the parameters should be qualitatively analyzed on a continuum to permit greater differentiation. The student should be helped in discovering that he or she does not just feel "great." He or she feels happy, cheerful, optimistic, elated, exhilarated, enthusiastic, lighthearted, blithe, carefree, vivacious, lively, or any one of the other more precise synonyms for his or her positive feeling of well-being.

### Table 1. Sample tabular format for comparison of village, town, and city across four parameters

|  | Village | Rating | Town | Rating | City | Rating |
|---|---|---|---|---|---|---|
| Employment opportunities | Agriculture | + | Agriculture, small business, light industry | + | Industry, manufacturing, commerce, service, merchandising | + |
| Educational institutions | One-room schoolhouse | – | Nursery schools, elementary schools, high schools | + | Nursery schools, elementary schools, academic and vocational high schools, business and technical colleges, universities | + |
| Pollution | Weed and grass fires | + | Automobiles, trucks, buses, industry | + | Automobiles, motorcycles, trucks, buses, manufacturing, coal, heating | – |
| Health services | Visiting nurse, doctor on call | + | Clinics (with several doctors), nurses, laboratory technician | + | Clinics, hospitals, nursing homes, general practitioners, specialists—surgeons, radiologists, etc. | + |

# Discussion of Divergent Responses

The discussion of divergent responses is necessary because the tasks are deceptively easy. Objects and concepts familiar to the students have purposely been chosen so that the emphasis in the tasks will be on the process of comparison. There are many possible answers, each of which seem to be equally correct. As an example, let us take the apple and orange from the first Page of the instrument. There will be few students who cannot recognize and express the differences between them. Answers may be based on physical aspects such as the type of skin and its color, and the texture, taste, smell, or color of the fruit. Another difference is that the orange is shown with a leaf and the apple is not. In addition, one can consider one's knowledge about the two different fruits. The two fruit can be compared according to their number of calories, vitamin content, or price. Without a specific goal for the comparison, all available information must be gathered comprehensively and as many perceptual and conceptual parameters as possible must be included.

When discussing students' responses, the best answer should be sought without rejecting any of the other answers. Without a specific goal for comparison, the labels "orange" and "apple" would be the best answer for the differences in the above example, since these labels denote all the respective attributes of these two fruits. It is true, however, and should be pointed out to the students, that the goal for comparison generates the parameters used in the comparison. The high vitamin C content of the orange becomes a critical factor in selecting a fruit for breakfast, while the color of the apple may be the relevant criterion for a fruit arrangement.

It is possible that all of the students may write the names of the fruit as their answer. The teacher must then ascertain whether this common answer is a product of reflection or the result of a happy accident. The teacher may list a number of inadequate parameters and ask why they were eliminated. Students must justify their answers in this instrument, as in all of the others.

## Place of Comparisons in the FIE Program

Because comparative behavior is an elementary building block for most cognitive processes, it is a function that must be enhanced before various other functions develop. Comparisons is, therefore, one of the first instruments introduced in Feuerstein's Instrumental Enrichment (FIE) program. Since the exercises in Comparisons provide the prerequisites for relational thinking and teach generalization and discrimination, they serve as a preparation for categorization, seriation, and syllogistic, analogical, and transitive thinking. Although there is an emphasis on comparative behavior throughout the FIE program, it is in this instrument that we foster an awareness of the importance of the comparative process, its meaning, and the techniques for its proper use.

## The Teacher as a Mediator

The teacher plays an extremely important role in the mediation of Comparisons, since merely solving the tasks will not result in the students' attainment of the goals set for the instrument. It is only through the teacher's mediation that the students gain insight into the transcendent nature and meaning of comparative behavior. In addition to the previously discussed regulation of behavior, fostering a feeling of competence, individuation, and independence, the teacher also provides mediation in other areas.

Through the exploration and discussion of different responses to the same question, the teacher helps to enhance the students' awareness of the relevance of the parameters and challenges the students to look for novel and creative solutions to everyday problems. For example, our language is rich in similes and metaphors. "It's like falling off a log," "It's like shooting fish in a barrel," "He has rocks in his head," and "She's a bleeding heart" are all common expressions. Once students have learned to compare, they enjoy analyzing similes in which two unlike things are joined. Finding the attributes that make two very different things similar provides a meaningful challenge. By seizing the opportunities for comparative behavior offered by subject matter and classroom interactions, the teacher both models the process and invokes the students' increased activity in comparing. Teachers mediate and encourage sharing behavior by offering a wide variety of personal examples of more sophisticated uses of comparative behavior.

By interpreting to the students the meaning of their responses and the progress they have made, the teacher mediates the feeling of competence and makes them aware of the changes that have taken place in their cognitive processes.

## Units in Teacher's Guide to Comparisons

Pages have been grouped with others that share similar objectives and principles. This has been done for purposes of analysis and discussion. Suggestions for teaching the individual Pages are included.

The Pages in this guide are arranged into the following units: Unit I: Cover Page–Page 6; Unit II: Pages 7–13; and Unit III: Pages 14–16.

## Use of Color

Color is expressed in two forms in the Pages in this guide—as an outline or as shading (stripes, crosshatching, or solid fill). By incorporating two colors, color automatically becomes a criterion for comparison even if it is irrelevant to the exercise. Color increases the number of variables for comparison by one. The question of whether or not color should be considered as a criterion for comparison is a question of relevance. It can act as an interference for those who consider it irrelevant; it can change the answer for those who consider it relevant.

## Abridged Version

An abridged version has been prepared for use with special populations on a prescriptive basis. It consists of two Pages of introduction to the tasks of the instrument and the following Pages for independent work: Page 4 (AV 1); Page 5 (AV 2); Page 9 (AV 3); Page 11 (AV 4); Page 12 (AV 5); and Page 14 (AV 6).

# Teacher's Guide to Comparisons

# UNIT I

## Objectives

To learn the strategy of comparison.

To find all the possible parameters that can be used in comparing.

To seek the most critical, most characteristic, and most relevant dimension as the basis for comparison.

To differentiate between objects along the continuum of a single parameter or as subsets of an inclusive set.

To practice comparisons in tasks that progress from the concrete to the abstract.

## Subgoals

To enrich the repertoire of concepts and labels by adding parameters for comparison with each task.

To use superordinate concepts to describe similarities and differences.

Cover Page–Page 6

# Analysis in Terms of the Cognitive Map

## Content

Comparison between two familiar objects, figures, or concepts. Relationship described in superordinate concepts.

## Modality

Figural, pictorial, and verbal.

## Phase

### Input

Clear perception of two elements in order to gather complete and precise information of all their attributes.

Use of appropriate concepts, labels, and terms to describe similarities and differences between objects and to discriminate between them.

Use of spatial and temporal concepts as parameters for comparison.

Systematic exploration of the various elements of the task.

Conserving the constancy of the objects of comparison across changes that may occur in one or more of their characteristics, such as size, quantity, color, orientation, and direction.

Use of two or more sources of information either from the items in two different frames, or two or more different attributes of the item in a single frame.

Precise input so that various characteristics are differentiated.

### Elaboration

Establishment of relationships between objects and events in terms of their similarities and differences.

Learning the techniques and strategies of comparison prior to spontaneous comparative behavior.

Selection of relevant attributes.

Using the products of comparison as a basis for inference and logical reasoning.

Summation of the attributes that are similar and/or different in order to evaluate and form judgments.

Forming categories on the basis of perceptual and semantic concepts by using criteria that are constant, critical, and relevant.

Seeking superordinate concepts on the basis of hypothetical thinking and logical evidence.

Use of visual transport or interiorization in the mental superimposition necessary for comparison.

### *Output*

Enriching the repertoire to allow precise communication of the products of comparison.

Restraint of impulsivity and deferring a response until all the information has been gathered and elaborated.

Precision in the selection of concepts that are sufficiently exclusive and/or inclusive to describe either similarities or differences.

## Operations

Discrimination; generalization; integration; seriation of attributes; analysis and ordering of a superordinate parameter.

## Level of abstraction

Low in tasks in which two pictures are compared. Medium in which labels for concrete objects are compared. High in tasks in which abstract concepts are compared.

## Level of complexity

Low.

## Level of efficiency

High on simplistic level. Low until anticipated difficulties are overcome as a result of learning and practice.

| Anticipated difficulties due to | Methods of eliminating, bypassing, or overcoming anticipated difficulties |
|---|---|
| Class difficulties in reading and writing. | Comparative behavior is so important that the instrument should not be delayed until the acquisition of competency in reading and writing. Tasks should be done orally, with teacher noting responses on board so they can be summarized, referred to, etc. |
| Inadequate or partial description of objects of comparison. | Brainstorm with the entire class to gather all of the information. Break class into small groups or pairs so that students learn from one another. |
| Itemization of dimension of each object separately instead of attempting to join them in a superimposition (e.g., on the left . . . on the right). | Use tables and charts to gather and summate information as shown in lesson on the Cover Page which follows. |
| Use of irrelevant parameters as the basis for comparison (e.g., giving "number" as the main difference between squares and triangles). | Make goal of comparison explicit. Discuss and practice the necessity of making differences the differentiators. |
| Impulsive response as a result of superficial scanning. | Model search and focus. Impose a latency period for scanning before allowing a response. Ask, "What else?" or "What about . . . ?" |
| Lack of superordinate concepts to describe commonality and/or difference. | Introduce "A and B are both . . ." Teach superordinate concepts and have students volunteer all subordinate concepts included in them. |
| Overgeneralization (e.g., two boys in task 1, Page 1, described as "humans"); undergeneralization (e.g., milk and salt defined as "objects"). | Use of Venn diagrams to indicate sets and subsets. Define and contrast meaning of concepts. Give examples of their appropriateness. |
| Global perception of concrete and abstract items (e.g., difference between television and movies). | Determine reason for lack of analysis. Appropriate scanning strategies can overcome difficulties in global perception of concrete objects. If lack of information is causing difficulty, provide it. The task is not testing knowledge. |

## Suggested Discussion Topics for Insight and/or Bridging

What are the differences between description and comparison (e.g., the Netherlands vs. the United States; poetry vs. prose)?

When we look at something, do we all see it exactly the same way (e.g., blind men and an elephant; witnesses in court)?

Can we compare things we cannot see (e.g., life in the Middle Ages and life in the twenty-first century; 2/16 and 1/8)?

Is what stands out (is salient) the most important attribute?

How much difference (or similarity) will our society tolerate?

What are some generalizations (laws, rules, sayings, proverbs) that we recognize? How did they become generally accepted?

# Cover Page

## Objectives

To introduce the instrument and its subject.

To introduce and define concepts necessary for comparing.

To find all the possible parameters for comparing two items.

## Vocabulary

| | | | |
|---|---|---|---|
| comparison | superimposition | identical | different |
| same | similar/dissimilar | alike | dimension |
| attribute | characteristics | resemble | parameter |
| orientation | opposite | figure | shape |
| position | color | size | location |
| relevant | irrelevant | critical | illusion |

## Mediation

Mediation for intentionality and reciprocity, transcendence and meaning is emphasized on the Cover Page with the introduction of the instrument. Mediation of an awareness of change is elicited in the discussion of the differences between the two parts of the symbol.

Cover Page

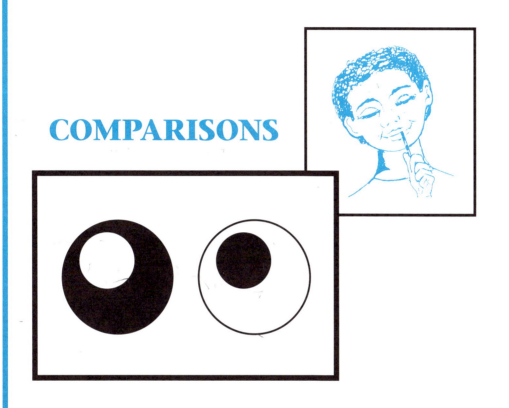

© 1995 by R. Feuerstein, Hadassah–Wizo–Canada Research Institute.

## Introduction and Discussion

1. Comparison of Cover Page with previous Cover Pages.

2. The act of comparing involves mentally superimposing one object over another to find where they overlap and where they do not (e.g., putting one thing over another to see if they are the same length).

3. In superimposing this Cover Page over those of the other instruments, we find that the boy in the upper right-hand corner and the motto are the same; the symbol, however, is different.

    a. Similar = One thing is like another; they share certain characteristics.

    b. Different = One thing is unlike another, set off from another, in certain characteristics.

---

**Comparison involves finding both similarities and differences. In things that are similar, there may be differences; in things that are different, there may be similarities.**

---

4. In comparing two Cover Pages, we find there are both similarities and differences. In comparing the boy and the motto on each Cover Page, we find no differences. They are identical.

5. Identity means there are no differences at all. Things are exactly and precisely the same in all attributes and details. When the objects are superimposed, there is a complete overlap.

    a. Identity is rare in nature; even any two snowflakes are different.

    b. Identity is the goal of quality control of all manufactured items (e.g., CDs, machine parts, printing or typed copy, packaging).

    c. Identity is sought in blueprints, recipes, and prescriptions.

    d. Weights and measures are identical (e.g., although a pound of feathers and a pound of steel weigh the same, their quantities are different).

6. Comparison of elements in the symbol: "Look at the symbol and tell us about it."

   (NOTE: The student's response will indicate whether or not he or she compares spontaneously and attempts to find relationships or whether he or she merely itemizes and describes each element separately.)

7. More detailed items require greater involvement to gather all the information (e.g., a complex sentence or map vs. a schematic sketch).

   a. Must scan since it is impossible to perceive all the details at a glance.

   b. Must move systematically from element to its counterpart in comparing two complex or detailed items.

8. When a comparison is not directed by a specific goal (e.g., to find out who is taller), the process starts with gathering all the possible data about each of two or more items, and then determining whether each characteristic of one item is the same as or different from that of the other.

   a. Characteristics = The qualities, attributes, or traits of an item. When we use a particular characteristic to compare, we will call it a parameter or criterion. (e.g., teacher is a human, female, woman, wife, mother, daughter, sister, granddaughter, swimmer. She is tall and large. She has dark hair and blue eyes. She was born in California. Her favorite sport is basketball. Student is a human, male, boy, son, grandson, brother. He is tall and thin. He has dark hair and dark eyes. He was born in Illinois. His favorite sport is soccer. Now we match characteristic to characteristic to see what is the same, different, or equivalent between the two, and the degree of difference, if it exists.)

   b. Equivalent = Has the same value or weight (e.g., son and daughter are equivalent in their place in the family, but opposite in gender; $1/2$ c. margarine = $1/2$ c. butter in recipes.)

9. List similarities and differences of items in the picture on the Cover Page using superordinate concepts. (Chart on board.)

| Item on left | Item on right | Concept | Similar | Different |
| --- | --- | --- | --- | --- |
| Round | Round | Shape | X | |
| Circles | Circles | Figure | X | |
| Two | Two | Number | X | |
| Black-white | Black-white | Color | X | |
| Large-small | Large-small | Size* | X | |
| Small in large | Small in large | Orientation | X | |
| White in black | Black in white | Color's location | | X (Opposite) |
| Left | Right | Position | | X (Opposite) |

*Although there may seem to be a difference in size, this is due to an optical illusion created by the difference in color. The illusion of different size created by different colors is used in clothes to make persons look thinner, and in painting to make a room look larger. Measuring will offer conclusive evidence of similarity in size.

Measurement = Process of ascertaining the extent, dimensions, quantity, etc., of something, especially by comparing it to a standard.

**Measurement always involves a comparison, but not all comparisons involve a measurement.**

10. We can decide how similar two things are by the number of attributes they share. (With most classes, it is premature to introduce the critical nature of some attributes in determining similarity/dissimilarity.)

11. Objects can be compared using all of their attributes, only a number of them, or just one, depending on the need.

    a. Comparison of $1/2$ and $1/4$ using one attribute: quantity.

    b. Comparison of two boxes of soap using two attributes: size and price.

c. Comparison of two candidates for office using many attributes: party, platform, intelligence, charisma, age, health, profession, etc.

12. Sometimes similarities and differences are very obvious (e.g., those on the Cover Page). Sometimes they require an investment of time and effort to find (e.g., blood tests; gas mileage and car maintenance costs; legal contracts; two characters in a story or play).

**Comparison is at the core of all of our decisions and judgments.**

13. Individual or small group assignments for application of principle:

    a. Give three examples of typical comparisons you might be called on to make in an academic or vocational subject, or in a life experience.

    b. Choose one of the following vocations: student, teacher, homemaker, bus driver, carpenter, typist, messenger. Give examples of ten comparisons the person of your choice might be called on to make in the course of an average day.

# Page 1

## Objectives

To find similarities and differences between two pictures.

To differentiate on the basis of what one perceives and what one knows.

To describe the commonality between two objects with a superordinate concept.

To describe the differences between two objects using the same parameter.

To introduce interclass and intraclass differences.

To enrich vocabulary both quantitatively and qualitatively.

## Vocabulary

| | | | |
|---|---|---|---|
| common | include | implicit | relative |
| continuum | exclude | appearance | set |
| superordinate | differentiate | salient | class |

## Mediation

Mediated regulation and control of behavior is needed for Pages 1 and 2 in tasks in which all available information must be gathered, elaborated, and the response expressed in one word. The transformations that occur between the two parts of the same task also must be mediated.

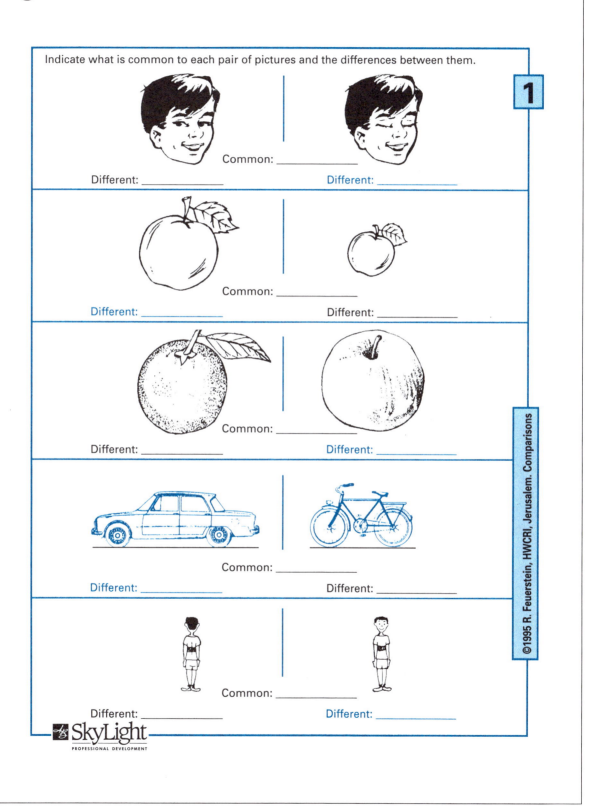

# Introduction and Discussion

1. A picture is a form of communicating and presenting information. We must "read" the picture to gather information on "who," "what," "when," "where," and even "why." A picture is worth a thousand words.

2. We can compare the things we perceive using the criteria we used on the Cover Page: shape, figure, color, number, size, orientation, location, and position.

**To what we see, we can add what we know and what we can infer. We can infer many things from what we know.**

(For example, we see an adult and several young people in a room. The young people are sitting at desks; the adult is standing next to a blackboard. We know this is a common arrangement for a classroom. We infer that the adult is the teacher and the youngsters are the students.)

3. We define the task by reading and understanding the instructions.

4. Implicit in the task is that commonality can be described by one word—a concept—that permits generalization and discrimination (inclusion and exclusion).

   a. Common = Belonging to or shaped by both items in the comparison; can be decided on the basis of perceptual or conceptual overlap (e.g., common interest, common rooms, common denominator).

   b. Concept = Class of "things" (objects, events, relations) that vary among themselves so we can tell the members apart, but are all grouped together and called by the same name.

   c. Generalization = Giving the same label to a new example that differs in some way from previously met examples; making the same response.

   d. Discrimination = Using a different label (making a different response) for an example that shares some, but not all, of the same properties with previous examples.

5. Overgeneralization should be avoided.

   a. In the first task, the commonality is boy (not boys), or even smiling boy. Vertebrates, mammals, humans, and males are all overgeneralizations. Whereas it is true that a boy is a subset and/or a member of all the previously mentioned sets and included in them, it is not true that all vertebrates, mammals, humans, and males are boys.

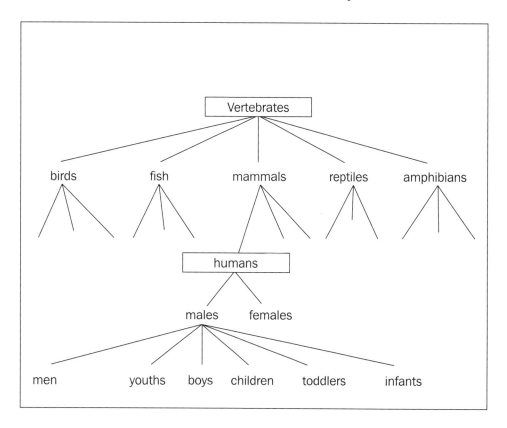

   b. In task 2, the commonality should be apples, not fruit or food.

6. Implicit in the task is that the differences should be expressed using two attributes. This can be inferred from the number of provided lines. The two words should represent different aspects of the same parameter.

   a. We can describe the bicycle in task 4 as having room for only one passenger and the auto as having four wheels, but that is a description, not a comparison.

b. We will arrive at a response by comparing. A comparison of the various attributes should read:

| Car | Bicycle |
|---|---|
| closed | open |
| four wheels | two wheels |
| many riders | one rider |
| storage in trunk | no storage space |
| horsepower | pedal power |
| weighs two tons | weighs about 30 pounds or less |
| gasoline engine | pedals |
| costs thousands | costs less than a hundred, unless special model |

7. It is implicit that the answers be short. This can be inferred from the amount of given space.

8. In three tasks we are given an object that differs from another in only one attribute. There is a constancy of the object over changes in the single attribute. Because there is only one difference, that difference is salient (stands out) in these particular tasks.

   a. Task 1: Difference: eyes open; eyes closed.

   The given information is not sufficient for the inference that the closed eyes indicate sleeping. Whereas most people close their eyes when they sleep, not all people whose eyes are closed are sleeping.

   b. Task 2: Difference: size.

   Because we have no way of knowing the absolute sizes of the apples without weighing or measuring, we must use size as a relative measure, one in relation to the other. If we were to draw a continuum of size, the two would be on opposite ends relative to each other. In comparing only two items according to a relative attribute, we are usually content with using opposites, but we are not limited to them. Finer discrimination requires the use of gradations between the two poles. Contrast large or small things with greater precision by using the following:

| miniscule | minute | wee | tiny | small | medium | large | gigantic | enormous |

Or instead of hot or cold, consider the following:

| icy | cold | cool | tepid | lukewarm | warm | hot | burning | boiling |

   c. Task 5: Difference: orientation (back and front).

   The boy is unchanged despite the transformation in his orientation.

9. There are other parameters according to which apples can be compared (color, shape, odor, taste, type, texture, firmness, blemishes, location of orchard, etc.), but since there is no way of definitively determining these parameters from the picture, they are not appropriate here.

10. In expressing the commonality between two different kinds of objects (different sets), we must gather all available information, and then seek the relationship between the two in terms of their overlap. The label will be the superordinate concept. Thus, apples and oranges are "fruit," not food.

11. Task 4: Commonality is "vehicles."

    Vehicles = Any means by which someone travels or something is carried or conveyed. It is a more precise and inclusive term than transport or means of transportation, which includes ships, airplanes, and railroads.

**We cannot see the commonality in the tasks in which the objects belong to different classes. We see the difference. Through a summation of the differences we arrive at the completion of the statement, "They are both . . ."**

12. The differences between the apple and orange that we see and know are many. Dimensions such as color, taste, size, shape, appearance, texture, etc., can be used to describe the differences, but provide only partial answers. The terms "apple" and "orange" denote all the attributes of the respective objects and denote all the differences. The labels "car" and "bicycle" similarly denote all the differences in task 4.

**In describing the differences between the two subsets of an inclusive set, the label of the subset should be used because it denotes all the attributes shared by members of the subset.**

13. Whereas many answers may be correct, there are some answers that are better than others.

    a. More precise—they do not include too much nor leave anything out.

    b. More relevant—for example, the characteristic of having a leaf is not constant and invariant for an orange. It is irrelevant to the quality of being an orange.

    c. More differentiating—for example, "tastes bad" as opposed to too tart, bitter, acidic, spicy, salty, or insipid, flavorless, etc., which differentiate elements of the same dimension, or prizefighter versus flyweight, bantamweight, featherweight, welterweight, lightweight, or heavyweight.

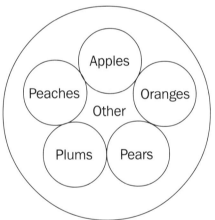

The Subsets of Fruit

**When no goal for a comparison is given, we must gather all the information and compare according to all the possible parameters.**

14. To our previous list of parameters for comparison, we can add set or class and subset. (There is no need as yet to differentiate between the concepts of "subset" and "set members.")

# Page 2

## Objectives

To compare items using the parameters of geometric configuration and shape, direction, number, and texture.

To introduce the concept of critical attributes.

## Vocabulary

| | | |
|---|---|---|
| geometric forms or figures | number | direction |
| intraclass differences | constancy | adjectives |

## Mediation

See Page 1.

# Page 2

Indicate what is common to each pair of pictures and the differences between them.

**2**

○ ○ ○ ○ | □ □ □ □

Common: _____
Different: _____   Different: _____

▽ ▽       △ △
▽ ▽       △ △ △
▽ ▽       △ △

Common: _____
Different: _____   Different: _____

Common: _____
Different: _____   Different: _____

Common: _____
Different: _____   Different: _____

Common: _____
Different: _____   Different: _____

© 1995 R. Feuerstein, HWCRI, Jerusalem. Comparisons

SkyLight
PROFESSIONAL DEVELOPMENT

© 1995 by R. Feuerstein, Hadassah–Wizo–Canada Research Institute.

# Introduction and Discussion

1. In comparing Page 2 to Page 1, we find a new modality—figural (e.g., a picture of a dress, a sketch, a pattern).

    a. Three tasks contain items that belong to the same class: geometric figures.

    b. The instructions, layout, and tasks are the same.

2. The two items to be compared in tasks 2, 3, and 5 resemble each other in all dimensions except one. It is the single thing that differentiates between each pair of items.

3. Number is not a critical attribute in describing commonality, although it may be included in the description as an auxiliary parameter (e.g., four geometric figures, six triangles).

4. Number may become an essential parameter in describing differences when all other dimensions are alike (e.g., task 3). Number or quantity can be critical to a cashier, a teacher on a field trip, a butcher, a math student, an architect, or a contractor.

5. The faint outline of the shape of the cat on the right reveals that it is the same as the cat on the left. This would not have been apparent if the clear outline and print of the cat were not given in the frame on the left.

    a. Sometimes a photocopy comes out blurred, fuzzy, or indistinct. We can correct this by comparing it to a clean copy.

    b. We can fill in a missing letter in a misprinted word without even being aware that it is missing by having a clear picture in our mind of what the word should be (closure).

---
**The act of comparing in itself makes us become aware of what might otherwise be overlooked.**

---

6. In task 5 we might infer that the car is British since the steering wheel is on the right, but it is not a relevant bit of information. The difference in appearance is due to its change in orientation.

7. A minor difference or a difference in just one part is meaningful and may be critical (e.g., same shoe, different size; same song, different key; same car, different lock; same phone number except for one digit).

8. Characteristics that may be irrelevant in some circumstances may become critical in others.

    a. Color: matching paint, dye, buttons. Find examples of when color is irrelevant.

    b. Direction: spelling, buses, reading music, right and wrong side of textured material. Find examples of when direction is irrelevant.

    c. Location: destination for a navigator, finding the right building in a housing complex, identifying a person in a picture. Find examples of when location is irrelevant.

9. Figures are easier to compare than either pictures or words because all of the extraneous information is removed and only the essentials are given. For example, contrast the ease of gathering information presented on graphs such as temperature, rainfall, and cost of living with gathering the same information from articles or pictures.

**Adjectives are generally used to describe the differences between members of the same class (intraclass differences), while nouns usually describe interclass differences. When the differences become the basis for the division of classes or sets into subsets, the subsets can be described in terms of use or function, power, source, etc.**

10. Relative and absolute differences can be contrasted (e.g., big-little vs. circle-square. Big-little can change without affecting the constancy of the object. Circle-square cannot change without changing the object itself).

# Page 3

## Objectives

To compare elements presented verbally.

To understand that words have a symbolic function.

To differentiate between the denotation and connotation of a word.

## Subgoal

To increase the repertoire of parameters for comparisons.

## Vocabulary

| | | |
|---|---|---|
| universal | emotion | idiosyncratic (individual, private) |
| specific | denote | symbolize |
| meaning | connote | signify |

## Mediation

Mediation of a feeling of competence is elicited by the use of a new modality. New situations and new contexts necessitate the mediation of meaning.

# Page 3

Indicate what is common to each pair of words and the differences between them.

Church } _____
Factory

Love } _____
Hate

Earring } _____
Ring

Bread } _____
Meat

Milk } _____
Coca-Cola

Movie theater } _____
Television

Baby } _____
Old man

# Introduction and Discussion

1. When comparing this Page to the previous one, note that the instructions and the task are the same. However, the modality (language of presentation) is different.

**Words are less concrete than pictures. Verbal modality is generally more universal.**

(Instead of a picture of a specific ring, we are presented with the word "ring," which symbolizes or stands in the place of the concept of rings.)

2. We can compare two actual objects, two pictures, two words that signify (are the sign for) objects, two ideas, or two relationships. These comparisons range from the concrete to the abstract.

3. In these tasks, we do not actually see the objects we are comparing. We work on the basis of what we have stored in our memory and can represent in our minds.

**By looking at the composition of a word, we cannot see either similarities or differences between the object it symbolizes and the object another word symbolizes; we can only compare their length, their spelling, their sound, etc.**

4. There are a number of possible ways to express a similarity (what is common). In this Page, superordinate concepts signifying universal sets will be needed since the given items are members of two different subsets.

5. A strategy for finding a similarity (what is common) is to say "A and B are both . . ."

6. Differences between two items can be expressed at various levels.

    a. Idiosyncratic (individual and private): for example, I might say, "A baby cries all the time and an old man groans all the time," because this describes a baby and an old man that I know.

b. Particular: for example, a specific church that has stained glass windows versus a particular factory that has no windows.

c. Universal: for example, part or all of the constant, invariant characteristics of the object, event, or relationship.

7. We use universal concepts to define all objects or events that belong together.

8. In the first and last tasks, we must avoid idiosyncratic answers—those that refer only to objects with which we alone are familiar (e.g., in the first task, the answer could be "building"; "structure" is an overgeneralization. If student answers, "place my mother goes" as common to the factory and to church—the answer is idiosyncratic). The answer should reflect the function or use of the two different buildings.

9. There may be problems with verbalizing the similarities and differences between familiar concepts (e.g., "I know it, but I can't say it").

10. Love and hate are both strong emotions. They have a direct object. They are found on opposite poles of the same continuum or axis.

    a. Love = Profoundly tender or passionate feeling; warm personal affection. The term is often conversationally misused. Like, admire, adore, respect, and worship are a few possible substitutes.

    b. Hate = Passionate and intense dislike. Can be replaced in conversation by dislike, detest, despise.

11. There may be problems with differentiating because we do not have sufficient knowledge (e.g., differences between movies and television require knowledge of the relative means of projection and transmission).

12. We must beware of undergeneralization (e.g., "milk comes from a cow"; "Coca-Cola comes from a can").

> **It is easier to compare things that we can see or with which we are familiar than to compare abstract ideas.**

13. One must think carefully and review alternatives before deciding on the best answer.

> **When working in the verbal modality, it is necessary to decode the word and to represent the thing it symbolizes in all its detail. Then, it is necessary to act on the representation as if it were present in the perceptual field.**

14. Although we have been seeking superordinate concepts and terms for classes to designate what is common, we must remember that our need generates the comparison. (For example, if we are planning the lunch beverage for a home economics class, we are more interested in the vitamins A and D that the drink provides than whether it is natural or artificial.)

15. It is necessary to support our responses with justifications.

# Segment of Lesson
# Page 3

### *Mediation of meaning*

Teacher: Who would like to draw a comparison between Page 3, which we shall deal with today, and Pages 1 and 2. Yes, Danny?

Danny: Here, like in Pages 1 and 2, we have to write down what is similar and what is different, but this time we are presented with words rather than pictures.

Teacher: Very true, Danny. Could you tell us, in one word, what the two Pages have in common?

Danny: The kind of exercise, or activity.

Teacher: Right, they have the activity in common. And in what way are they different? Try to use one word.

Danny: How can I use one word to say that instead of pictures we have words?

Teacher: Pictures, words, numbers, drawings, and symbols (writes on the blackboard) all have a common use. What is the function of all of these? Please, Mildred.

Mildred: To say all sorts of things; to convey information.

Teacher: Very good, Mildred. Every one of these forms of conveying or presenting information is called a language or a modality (writes on the board). So how can we sum up our comparison of the two Pages? Yes, Ann.

Ann: They have the activity in common, but they differ in modality.

Teacher: Excellent. Let us now take the first pair of words. What do a church and a factory have in common? John.

John: They are both buildings.

Teacher: Very true. But is the fact that they are buildings their most important and most essential common attribute?

John: Yes, I think it is.

Teacher: You know class, near my neighborhood, there is a factory that manufactures bricks. It has a big sign that reads: Benedict Brown's Brick Factory. However, all the activity in this factory takes place in a big yard, in the open air, and not even the smallest building is present. Should this not be considered a factory? Yes, Robert.

Robert: Yes, but most factories are in buildings.

Teacher: This is true, Robert. But if factories that are not in buildings are also considered factories, then perhaps factories have some other common attribute which is more critical or essential. Yes, Jerry.

Jerry: Perhaps, they should be called places where people manufacture things.

Teacher: Excellent, Jerry. This is indeed a more essential attribute. Except that we cannot relate this attribute to churches also. Let's take a look at the list of words I'm writing on the blackboard: church, factory, school, public library, sports center, youth club, municipal center, hospital—how can we refer to all of these with just one word, one concept? Yes, Mary.

Mary: I think I know what you mean, but I can't say it.

Teacher: Well, we can refer to all these words as organizations or institutions. (Writes on the blackboard.)

# Page 4

## Objective

To compare items and abstract concepts on the basis of power, function, role, use, and physical attributes.

## Vocabulary

arbitrary    consensus    denotation    connotation

## Mediation

Mediation of challenge is necessary in the elaboration of the responses to the very difficult comparisons on this Page. Individuation and psychological differentiation are mediated in the discussion of the divergent responses to the task.

# Page 4 (AV 1)

Indicate what is common to each pair of words and the differences between them.

**4**

- Milk } _____  _____
- Salt       _____

- Sun } _____  _____
- Lamp     _____

- Ugly } _____  _____
- Wicked   _____

- Newspaper } _____  _____
- Magazine      _____

- Swimming pool } _____  _____
- Ocean              _____

- Lake } _____  _____
- River    _____

- Father } _____  _____
- Mother   _____

©1995 R. Feuerstein, HWCRI, Jerusalem. Comparisons

## Introduction and Discussion

1. The comparisons on this Page are difficult because the items for comparison are complex.

2. Words are arbitrary signs for labeling objects, concepts, and relationships. They convey these objects, concepts, and relationships in time and space.

3. To be effective for communication, words must denote the same thing to both speaker and listener. The definition of terms is a preliminary step in any argument.

4. Different cultures, different time periods, and different parts of the country assign different meanings to words (e.g., bread = food; bread = money; bread and water = starvation diet).

5. Words also connote different things to each of us as a result of our personal experiences.

6. In order to agree on similarities and differences, words must have identical meanings to each of us, and our need for comparing them must be the same.

7. Familiarity with items does not make their comparison easier.

    a. Despite the fact that "milk" and "salt" are very familiar, it is difficult to compare them.

    b. If we compare only the actual words, "milk" and "salt," we notice that both have four letters, with an "l" in the third place.

8. In order to compare, one must superimpose one item over the other. The degree of overlap may be very small, in which case the differences are greater than the similarities.

9. Without a model for comparison and a goal to orient the activity, all available information must be gathered and translated into parameters for comparison.

10. We can compare on the basis of the following:

    *Relative attributes:* unmeasured size, height, weight, width, length, breadth, depth, thickness, brightness, uncounted number, composition, taste.

*Spatial dimensions:* location, position, orientation, direction, side.

*Temporal dimensions:* sequence, order of precedence, seasons, time, year, day, hour.

*Function:* use, role, power, magnitude, intensity, source.

*Relationships:* opposites, part-whole, synonyms, identity, equivalency.

*Values:* legality, validity, desirability, morality.

*Aesthetics:* pretty-ugly, soothing-exciting, appealing-repelling.

*Absolute dimensions:* age, number, form, figure, temperature, color, measured size, measured weight, measured depth, measured thickness, transparency.

*Character or personality:* pleasant-unpleasant, sophisticated-naive, talkative-silent, intelligent-stupid, agreeable-disagreeable.

# Pages 5–6

*Note:* Pages 5 and 6 are taught together.

## Objectives

To describe similarities and differences using superordinate concepts.

To enhance flexibility in the use of concepts.

## Vocabulary

thickness     width     divergent     convergent     superordinate

## Mediation

A feeling of competence is mediated in tasks in which both the commonality and the difference are expressed using superordinate concepts. Mediation for the regulation of behavior is indicated in several of the tasks in which the given information must be explored and elaborated for the most appropriate response. In addition, there is mediation for individuation and psychological differentiation in three tasks in which the responses will diverge.

# Page 5 (AV 2)

In one word, indicate what is common to both pictures. Choose one word to describe the difference between them.

**1**

Common: _____
Different: _____

**2**

Common: _____
Different: _____

**3**

Common: _____
Different: _____

**4**

Common: _____
Different: _____

## Page 6

In one word, indicate what is common to both pictures. Choose one word to describe the difference between them.

**5**

Common: _____
Different: _____

**6**

Common: _____
Different: _____

**7**

Common: _____
Different: _____

**8**

Common: _____
Different: _____

# Introduction and Discussion

1. Compare these Pages with the first four Pages.

    a. Earlier, we had a combination of modalities; here, we have only the pictorial.

    b. In the first Pages, similarities were described by two words using the same parameter. In these Pages, a one-word, superordinate concept is used to describe the differences as well as the similarities.

2. In some tasks (1, 2, 5, 6, 7, and 8), similarities and differences are easily perceived.

    a. Responses will be convergent.

    b. Responses will only differ in the label given to the phenomenon.

3. The same phenomenon can be described in different ways. For example, in task 1, the difference may be described as follows:

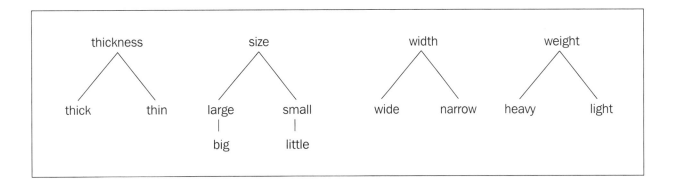

4. Alternative answers should be evaluated. For example, thickness refers to the number of pages in the book and is the best answer without a directed comparison.

5. Tasks 3 and 4 will have divergent responses.

    a. Inasmuch as no goal has been provided for the comparison, all the parameters should be considered before deciding on a response.

b. The strategy should be to start with the similarity, and then to ask in what or how the two similar objects differ.

c. The discussion should reveal that, in these tasks (3 and 4), the difference in color is irrelevant.

6. Differences should be directly associated with the given similarity, if possible, as a preparation for categorization.

   a. In task 3, if the similarity is described as workers, the differences between the given examples can be labeled as follows: sex—female or male; place—indoors or outdoors; activity—cooking or gardening; and tools—spoon and pot or hoe.

   b. Divergent responses will also be given for task 4 and can be labeled speed, means, care, etc.

**To arrive at superordinate concepts for differences, one must summate the differences and find a term that includes all objects of comparison. The differences must still be sought along the same parameter.**

7. Return to the first Pages and label the differences using a superordinate concept.

8. Find and discuss other examples in which differences are not visible such as:

   Two books: different authors, subjects, formats.
   Two basketball players: different positions, skills, speed, height.
   Two tests: different subjects, difficulty, results.
   Two teachers: different methods, subjects, training.
   Two brothers: different personalities, ages, temperaments.

# Teacher's Guide to Comparisons

# UNIT II

## Objectives

To compare objects to each other or to a standard in order to find similarities and/or differences based on several parameters simultaneously.

To construct examples similar to and different from a given standard, according to several criteria applied simultaneously.

To decipher written instructions and translate them into a motor act.

To rank given examples with varying degrees of similarity according to their proximity to a model.

## Pages 7–13

# Analysis in Terms of the Cognitive Map

## Content

Complex figures, simultaneously compared on several dimensions.

## Modality

Figural, with a minimum of pictorial and verbal elements.

## Phase

### Input

Precise perception of details of the model and an analytic perception of the whole's component parts.

Recognition and identification of transformations that occur, while conserving constancy of the figures.

Systematic exploratory behavior, using a search strategy.

Use of temporal dimensions to establish a plan for work and to sequence.

Selection of key words in the instructions and understanding their implications; use of labels as mediators for interiorization of complex figures.

Simultaneous use of several parameters, especially in construction tasks.

### Elaboration

Ability to keep in mind a great number of parameters during the process of elaboration.

Making a plan that will take into account the complexity of the tasks.

Use of hypothetical thinking and hypothesis testing to evaluate the response.

Selection of relevant cues as reference points.

***Output***

Deferring the response until all the data have been gathered and elaborated.

Evaluating the response for precision, accuracy, and completeness.

## Operations

Recognition; identification; construction; representation; seriation; differentiation; discrimination.

## Level of abstraction

Low.

## Level of complexity

Medium to high in Pages 12 and 13.

## Level of efficiency

Medium to high on all Pages but 12 and 13, in which it is very low. Pages 9 and 11 also may be difficult for some students.

| Anticipated difficulties due to | Methods of eliminating, bypassing, or overcoming anticipated difficulties |
|---|---|
| Inability to translate written instructions into a motor act (especially on Pages 12 and 13). | Ask students to paraphrase instructions. Define the task and what is given. Seek legitimate inferences. |
| Difficulty working independently. | Introduce strategies for checking work. Model systematic search, hypothetical thinking, and use of logical evidence. |
| Confusion between part-whole, form-size, size-area, direction-color, gestalt of figure (especially on Page 9). | Define each parameter, giving examples to enhance understanding. Discuss troublesome tasks with the class to be sure that if they did not seem confused, they did in fact differentiate and eliminate inadequate responses after reflection. |
| Disequilibrium caused by tasks that don't require a response. Disequilibrium caused by tasks that present an infinite number of options. | Analyze with the students the elements of the task that delimit the possible responses. Assist the students in breaking a complex task into its parts. Discuss with the students the legitimacy of divergent responses. |

# Suggested Discussion Topics for Insight and/or Bridging

When is "nearly" not enough (e.g., prescriptions, baking a cake, matching yarn to complete a sweater)?

Creating our own reference points and models.

Correct reading of cues (e.g., crying from joy or grief, looking at one's watch to see whether it is early or late, yawning from boredom or fatigue).

Culture-created cues and ways of looking at the world.

Inferences from products of comparison (e.g., if Venezuela is closer to the equator than Jerusalem, it will be warmer in Venezuela than in Jerusalem).

Importance of the difference: in appearance (7 + 3 vs. 7 x 3 vs. 7 – 3); in results (butter vs. motor oil in cooking); in language (homophone vs. homonym); in sound (fire drill vs. class period bell).

# Page 7

## Objectives

To find two identical objects from among five pictures.

To develop a search strategy.

To analytically perceive the object of a search.

## Subgoals

To internalize the attributes of the object.

To turn cues into points of reference.

## Vocabulary

| | | |
|---|---|---|
| exception | reference point | complex |
| vertical | horizontal | cue |

## Mediation

Mediation of goal-seeking, goal-setting, goal-planning, and goal-achieving behavior is necessary for tasks in which the identity of two items must be established. Strategies for search and evaluation of the response must be determined.

# Page 7

Place an X beneath the two pictures that are identical in each row.

**7**

# Introduction and Discussion

1. Review the definition of identity as being exactly and precisely the same in all attributes, with no differences.

2. There is no model given, so arbitrarily select a starting point (e.g., trying to find any two matching napkins from among many; looking for any two socks that are identical).

3. Scan the entire field until the task is complete.

4. Eliminate those that are obviously different (exceptions), thus narrowing the field of search (e.g., in looking up a word in the dictionary, eliminate all the sections in which the first letter of the word differs).

5. Notice the fact that color may be relevant to the process of identifying similar objects. For example, in the third task, the third and fourth pictures are not identical but are distinguished from the rest by color.

6. Plan the search strategy.

    a. Focus on one part of the object or on one attribute to serve as a model. Use it as a reference point in place of the whole, which is difficult to internalize.

    b. Select ears pointing left and color as cues for the rabbit on the far left. The fourth rabbit matches but is oriented differently. Move to the second rabbit and select its tail as a cue. The same tail is found on the rabbit on the far right. Check the second and the last rabbit, point by point, to ensure their identity.

    c. Rows 6 and 7 are the most difficult because of the quantity of their parts. Their solutions require a definition of the relationship among the various elements of the items.

**Strategies must be changed when they are not effective.**

7. Obvious differences must be eliminated to narrow field of search.

   a. In row 6 eliminate #3 because of the diagonal's orientation and #4 because the two inside figures face in the same direction. Select the fact that the left house is on top of the diagonal as a cue. This is not repeated. Move on to next figure. The corner of its house is beneath the diagonal. This is repeated in the last figure. Now check all the other attributes to verify identity.

   b. The position of the circle in row 7 is nondiscriminating because it appears in four of the figures. The L is almost totally inside the square only in the first figure. Change the cue to an overlapping L on the right side of the square as in the second figure.

### Identity can be critical.

*Examples:* driver's license; maps; matching material, buttons, screws, parts of motor; cutting patterns; weighing and measuring; timing; synchronization of watches.

# Page 8

## Objectives

To use either similarities or differences to rank objects according to their proximity to the model.

To use a code to designate rank order.

## Vocabulary

| proximity | code | order |
| distance | rank | sequence |

## Mediation

Mediation of an awareness of change is required in ranking tasks in which minute differences between items must be detected. In mediation for individuation and psychological differentiation, the teacher must acknowledge the legitimacy of the students' varied attitudes and approaches, even when they differ from his or her own.

# Page 8

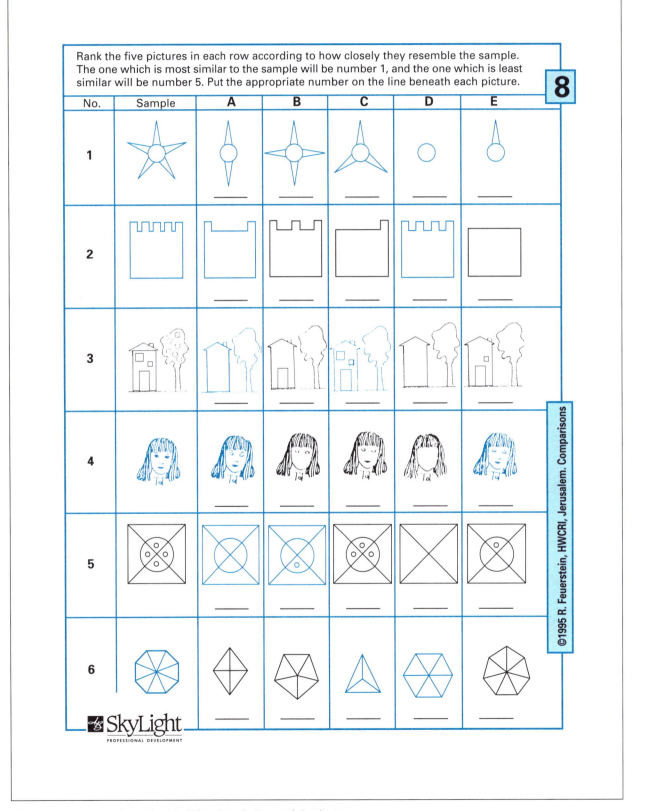

## Introduction and Discussion

1. Read instructions and look at Page in order to define task.

2. Use and define the different meanings of "close" (e.g., "Put your chair close to the wall"; "We are close friends"; "There is a close resemblance between the brothers"; "That was a close shave").

3. A close resemblance is not identity but rather a similarity in a large number of attributes.

4. Ranking is ordering according to some criterion. Low to high, or vice versa (e.g., Army rank, ranking of tennis players, test grades).

5. Plan a strategy.

    a. Define the model in terms of its attributes.

    b. Scan the various frames.

    c. It is easiest to recognize the one that is the most different. However, in a task with many items to inspect, this is not always the most economical and efficient way to work since it involves inspecting all the items with each decision.

6. We are asked to use a code (numbers) to indicate the degree of proximity.

    a. Various kinds of codes are used by manufacturers. They can indicate kind, quality, price, data, etc.

    b. As computer use increases, more and more things are codified.

    c. Some codes have complex meanings (e.g., designating eggs as Grade A refers to their size, color, and degree of freshness).

**We rank from high to low or from low to high. The ranking can be read from either direction.**

7. The degree of similarity that is required or that can be tolerated depends on the needs of the task.

a. Nuts must be exact in size and threads in order to fit their bolts. No differences can be tolerated.

b. Any paper will do for scratch paper.

c. If standard salad ingredients are not at hand, other fresh vegetables or fruit can take the place of the salad.

8. Compare this Page with Page 7 in terms of similarities and differences. Describe them in terms of their objectives.

# Segment of Lesson
# Page 8

### *Mediation for individuation and psychological differentiation*

Teacher: Who would like to read the instruction on the top of the Page? Gail.

Gail: (Reads instructions.)

Teacher: Right. And how will you be able to determine how close to the sample they are? Yes, Frank.

Frank: By comparing each picture to the sample and defining in what way they are alike and in what way they are different.

Teacher: Very good. And now please do the exercises on the Page.

Teacher: (A few minutes later.) Well, now let's check whether we've ranked all the pictures correctly. Who is going to rank the pictures of the first exercise? Sandy.

Sandy: The sample in the first exercise is a star with five points and, therefore, I've ranked picture B as number 1, picture C as number 2, A as number 3, E as number 4, and D as number 5.

Teacher: Very good, Sandy. And who would like to rank the pictures in the second exercise, the one with the wall. Yes, James.

James: D—1, B—2, A—3, C—4, and E—5.

John: Just a minute. I have ranked the pictures differently and I think my ranking is the correct one.

Teacher: How can the pictures be ranked differently, John?

John: Picture B should be 1, A—2, D—3, C—4, and E—5.

Teacher: James, would you please explain to John why you ranked the pictures the way you did?

James: Very simple. The wall in the sample has five bulges and therefore picture D, in which the wall has four bulges should be number 1. Picture B, in which the wall has three bulges should be number 2 and so on until picture E in which the wall has no bulges and which is therefore ranked number 5.

John: Wait a minute, James. You considered only the number of bulges in each wall. But if, in addition to the number of bulges, we take into account their location, we would realize that the wall in picture B is closer to the sample than the one in picture D. If we had to make both pictures identical to the sample, we would only have to add two bulges to the wall in B, whereas the wall in D would need both one additional bulge and a change in the location of two others.

Teacher: Excellent, John. You came up with another possible solution. What determines the ranking is the criteria that we choose and therefore different criteria will produce a different order. So both James' and John's ranking are perfectly correct. Any other ideas?

Clare: I think A should come before B. A and D are blue like the sample and so they should rank before the others. D would be first because its number of bulges is closer to the model, and A would be second. Then, I would finish by ranking B—3, C—4, and E—5, according to their number of bulges.

Teacher: Very good, Clare. When we consider color as a criteria for comparison, we have two groups—blue and black. Blue objects, in this case, rank higher than black. Then, within each group, we rank by the number of bulges.

# Pages 9 and 11

*Note:* Although each Page should be taught separately, they are presented together since they have many elements in common.

## Objectives

To compare objects to a given standard according to a number of given parameters; seeking similarities (Page 9) and differences (Page 11).

To define precisely the meaning of the various parameters and eliminate the confusion among them.

## Subgoal

To seek the relevance of the tasks for academic and life experiences.

## Vocabulary

| key words | size | shape |
| part-whole | area-size | figure-form |
| form-size | direction | color |

## Mediation

An opportunity for mediated regulation and control of impulsive behavior is provided in tasks in which a number of given parameters must be discriminated among. A feeling of competence is mediated to the students by discussing strategies for the solution of the tasks. Goal-setting and goal-achieving behavior must also be mediated.

# Page 9 (AV 3)

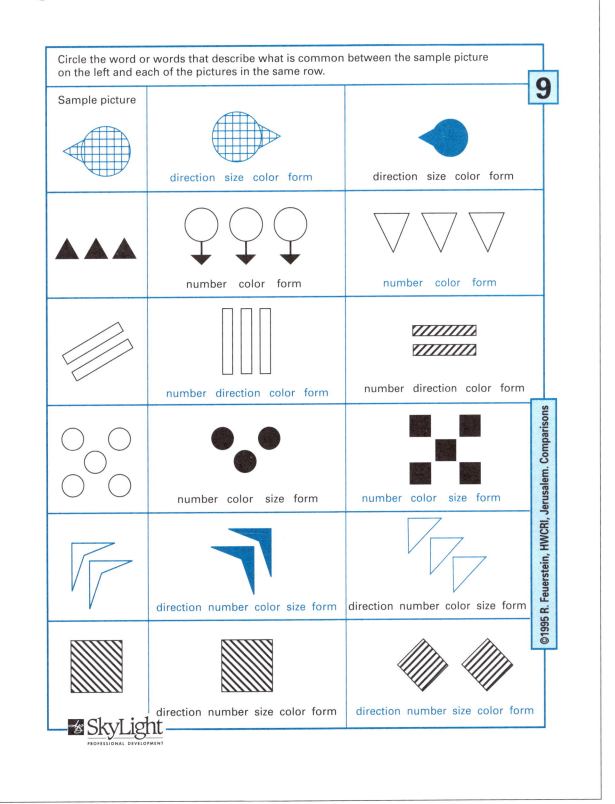

# Page 11 (AV 4)

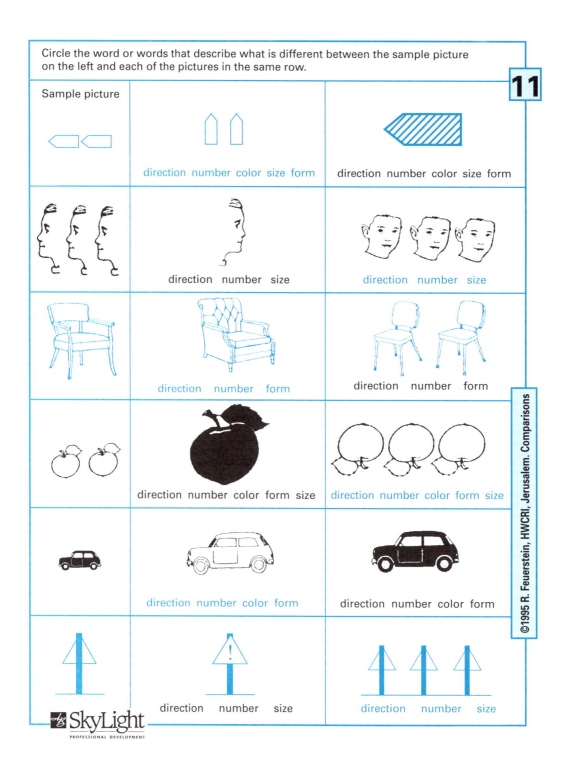

## Introduction and Discussion

1. Read the instructions, paraphrase them, and define the task.

   a. The key words are "circle," "sample," "each picture," "common" (Page 9), and "different" (Page 11).

   b. The instructions imply that the words that are not circled will be different on Page 9 and similar on Page 11.

2. Make a plan and decide on a strategy for solving tasks.

   a. Look at the model figure. Describe it fully to yourself.

   b. Use a universal label if there is one (e.g., triangle, circle, square, rectangle, apple, boy, chair, car, highway sign).

   c. Label by association if a universal label is not available (e.g., bird head, arrowhead, bullets). For example, call a person "Mr. Jones" if you know his name. You may call him "the man who looks like a stork" if you do not.

   d. Add appropriate adjectives to aid in interiorization (e.g., "checkered" bird head, "black" triangle, etc.).

   e. Transport the model visually, using interiorization or verbal mediators, to each picture and superimpose it.

   f. The word(s) describing the area of overlap is circled on Page 9. The word(s) that describes what is not included in the overlap is circled on Page 11.

   g. Check work by translating what is circled into a sentence. Then say the sentence while looking at the model.

   *Page 9, task 1:* The size, color, and form of the bird head in picture 1 are the same as those in the model. The direction is different. In picture 2, the direction and form of the bird head are the same. The size and color are different.

   *Page 11, task 1:* In picture 1, the direction of the bullet is different than in the model. In picture 2, the number, color, and size are different. The direction and form are the same.

### The constancy of the object is conserved despite changes in one or more of its attributes.

(For example, same person despite change in clothes, role, position, action, mood, time of day, place, manners, or activity.)

3. Great care must be taken to be precise in defining the meaning of the parameters.

    a. Confusion between size and form in Page 9, task 1. Size is measurable; form is synonymous here with shape.

    b. Confusion between size and form may cause reading difficulties when the constancy of a word is lost because its size or type style differs from the familiar.

    c. A part may mistakenly stand for the whole, as in task 2, Page 9. This becomes apparent when some students react to a small, black triangle at bottom of circle as if it were the black triangle of the model.

    d. Part-whole difficulties may cause reading problems when two words are confused because the first two or three letters of the second word are the same as those of a familiar word.

    e. Global perception of a gestalt may cause the model to be viewed as a single form (similar to the dots on a domino) instead of as a number of separate elements, each related to one another in a certain way (Page 9, task 4). Perhaps the problem would not occur if "orientation" were included as a parameter. In a diagnosis of the source of the problem, the consistency of the response should be checked. If a student responds to the gestalt (Page 9, task 4), the number will be different and the form the same in picture 1; the number will be the same and the form different in picture 2.

    f. There may be confusion between size and area in tasks 4 and 5, Page 9. Only the size of like objects can be measured and compared. To compare unlike objects, the dimensions of each must be transformed into area. In these tasks, however, we are satisfied with a rough estimate of the relative amount of space the two figures occupy.

g. Illusion of size difference is created by color in task 5, Page 9. The blue arrowhead looks larger than the white one. The illusion of the difference can be corrected by superimposition or measurement.

h. Stripes can either be considered as a color or as integral component of an object (e.g., stripes woven into material as opposed to being printed on the surface). The definition of color as one or the other will obviously make a difference in the description of the orientation of an object. The change in the direction of the stripes in task 6, Page 9, can be described as a change in orientation or direction if they are considered a part of the object; otherwise, the transformation can be described as a change in color.

**The relevancy of differences between objects is a function of the need that generated the comparison.**

(For example, neither height, weight, sex, hair and eye color, age, place of birth, marital status, nor food preferences are meaningful differences in selecting a substitute for a math teacher.)

4. There are obvious differences between the two black cars in task 5, pictures 1 and 3, Page 11, yet none of the given parameters can be circled. The difference in size or distance from the observer is not considered a relevant parameter by which to compare them.

5. The discussion of insight on Page 9 should focus on the importance of the similarities among objects, despite the differences between them.

*Examples:* Despite differences in age, sex, appearance, residence, major interest, experience, skill, etc., all the members of the vocational class are vocational students. The application of a law or rule is based on the similarity of the crime (e.g., traffic tickets, library fines, demerits). Words are spelled and written the same way, despite differences in handwriting, sentence construction, or subject matter.

6. The discussion for insight on Page 11 should focus on the importance of differences among objects, despite any similarities (e.g., looking for a car in the parking lot or for seats in a theater; differences in amount of money, indicated by the place of the decimal point; differences in symptoms for different illnesses; difference in appearance to tell people apart; difference in sound of motor to indicate what is wrong with it; different ranks among members of the army, navy, or marines).

7. We can look for similarities and differences between a given model and something else, or between a model that exists only in our imagination and something else (e.g., the kind of girlfriend or boyfriend we want; the appearance of what we are making and our mental picture of how it should look, taste, sound, or feel; an article of clothing that we can visualize but cannot exactly describe).

**The basis for generalization is similarity. The basis for discrimination is difference.**

# Page 10

## Objectives

To locate and describe five differences between two pictures.

To search systematically according to a strategy.

## Subgoal

To practice precise perception, systematic search, visual transport, labeling, establishment of relationships, and restraint of impulsivity.

## Vocabulary

| | | |
|---|---|---|
| eaves | hypothesis | texture |

## Mediation

Mediation of an awareness of change is elicited by tasks that require comparison of two pictures that differ only in five aspects. The change or transformation from picture to picture must be noted and labeled.

# Page 10

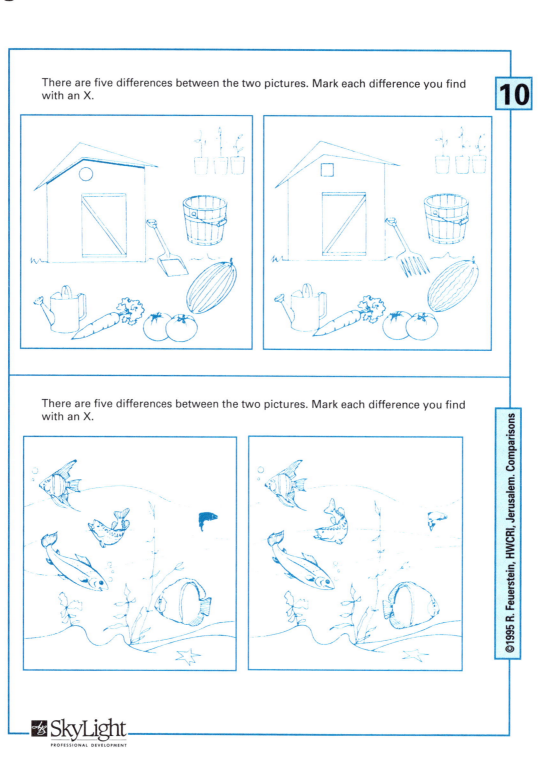

## Introduction and Discussion

1. Definition of the task limits the search and defines the experience.

2. In order to ascertain the differences, we must also look for the similarities. We narrow the field of search by eliminating the similarities.

3. The task requires systematic search. It is necessary to draw an imaginary line to divide the picture and scan from left to right, from right to left, or from top to bottom.

4. Another strategy is to focus on a part and transport it visually or through verbal mediators to the other picture and its counterpart (e.g., here the window is round, there the window is square).

5. Since there is no model, there is no right and wrong, only differences.

6. We know there are five differences. When we have found them, we can stop looking; we have completed the task.

7. For communication and easy comparison of completed work, it is efficient to number and label, as well as to mark each difference with an X.

8. Top of Page: Interclass differences

|   | Picture on left | Picture on right | Concept |
|---|---|---|---|
| 1. Roof line (eaves) | Double | Single | Number |
| 2. Window | Round (circular) | Square | Shape or form |
| 3. Line on door | Upper left to lower right | Lower left to upper right | Direction |
| 4. Tool | Shovel | Pitchfork | Type or function |
| 5. Watermelon | Straight lines | Wavy lines | Color or texture |

Summary: Differences in number, orientation, shape, type of tool, and gross differences in appearance.

9. Bottom of Page: Intraclass differences

   The lines drawn in the picture have a double function: to aid the systematic search by dividing the field, and to serve as a reference for positions of the fish. The task involves scanning and focus.

|  | Picture on left | Picture on right | Concept |
|---|---|---|---|
| 1. Fish orientation | Mouth above line 2 | Mouth below line 2 | Orientation |
| 2. Fish color | Blue | White | Color |
| 3. Fish mouth in "section" 4 | Open | Closed | Position |
| 4. Fish direction | Facing left | Facing right | Direction |
| 5. Starfish arms | Six | Five | Number |

   Summary: Differences are fine and require discrimination between parts of wholes.

10. Conclusion

   **When two things are supposed to be identical, yet there are differences between them, we can assume that one of them is wrong. To discover which of the two is incorrect, we must refer to an objective third source.**

   (For example, if we have two different spellings for the same word, we need to look in the dictionary to see which is correct; if we have two telephone numbers for the same person, one of which contains a transposition of numbers, we need to look in the phone book, ask information, or ask the person whose phone number it is.)

# Pages 12–13

*Note:* Pages 12 and 13 are the most difficult Pages in this instrument. They should be taught separately. They are presented together because they share common elements.

## Objectives

To construct items that are similar to (Page 12) and different from (Page 13) the model based on a variety of parameters.

To follow instructions precisely.

To use hypothetical thinking, inference, and logical evidence to complete a task successfully.

## Subgoal

To discriminate among stable and relative attributes.

## Vocabulary

| | | | |
|---|---|---|---|
| ambiguous | synchronous | restriction | contradict |
| unambiguous | sequence | assumption | |

## Mediation

Mediation of challenge is elicited by the highly novel and complex tasks on these Pages. Regulation and control of behavior needs to be mediated to ensure sufficient investment to gather and elaborate the necessary information. Goal-setting, goal-planning, and goal-achieving behavior is indicated in translating the verbal instructions into operations and strategies. Individuation and psychological differentiation are mediated in relation to the many different responses. Finally, a feeling of competence is mediated by interpreting to the student the meaning of the changes that have occurred in the course of his or her performance.

## Page 12 (AV 5)

Look at the sample. In each of the two frames, make a drawing that is the same as the sample only in those aspects indicated by the encircled words.

| Sample picture | Picture 1 | Picture 2 |
|---|---|---|
| (striped triangle) | number  color  (size)  (form) | (number)  color  size  (form) |
| (four black dots) | (number)  (color)  size  form | number  color  (size)  (form) |
| (three arrows pointing right) | direction  (number)  size  (form) | direction  number  size  form |
| (four squares) | color  (number)  size  (form) | (color)  (number)  size  form |
| (vertical rectangle) | direction  number  color  size  (form) | direction  number  color  size  form |
| (black rhombus) | number  color  (size)  (form) | (number)  (color)  size  (form) |

© 1995 R. Feuerstein, HWCRI, Jerusalem. Comparisons

# Page 13

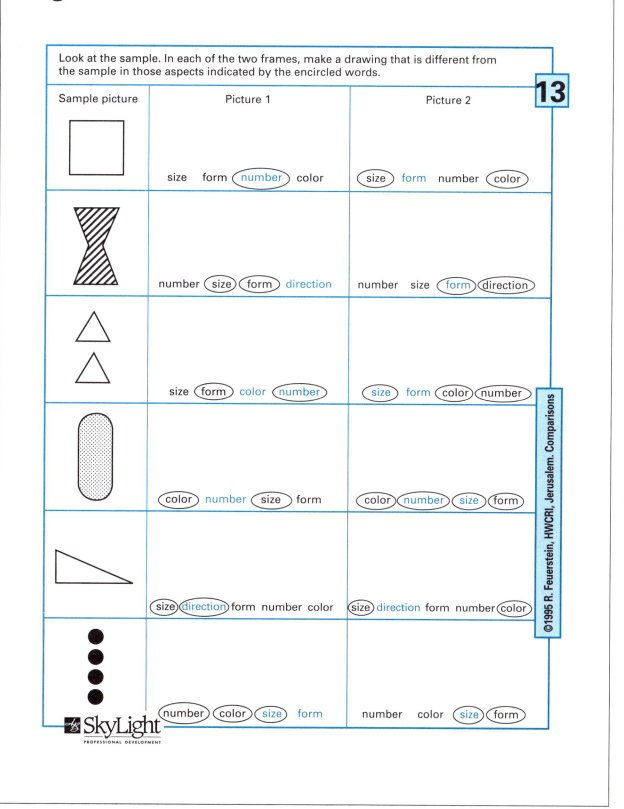

## Introduction and Discussion

1. Define the task by decoding the instructions. Then, decide how to translate verbal instructions into a motor act by sketching and drawing.

2. Discuss the meaning of the word "only."

   a. "Only" is underlined for emphasis and to attract attention. The use of italics, the size of the type, the kind of print, the color of ink, and spacing are other techniques for attracting attention in print.

   b. The word "only" is restrictive (e.g., "Entrance restricted to members only").

3. On the basis of hypothetical thinking, we assume that everything not circled in the tasks on Page 12 will be different: If a drawing must be similar to the model "only" in the circled dimensions, we can assume that the attributes that are neither circled nor mentioned *must* be different. Otherwise, there would be a similarity in those dimensions as well, which would contradict the instructions.

   Example: "I want a shirt similar to the one in the window only in style and color. I want a different size and short sleeves." Only the style and color should be similar. What about the material and the price? According to the stated request, they too should be different; however, because people usually are not precise, it would be better to ask.

4. The instructions on Page 13 are more ambiguous since they do not include the word "only" and there are no other cues. There are two possibilities:

   a. The drawings will certainly differ by the circled attributes. There may or may not be a difference in the other attributes.

   b. Circled attributes will be different. Attributes that are not circled will be the same.

### When instructions are ambiguous, we must decide what they imply and explore alternative ways of completing them.

5. Logically, there would be no reason to circle any of the attributes if they could all be different. The only reason to circle some is to differentiate them from others that would be the same.

6. Compare Page 12 to Page 9. (Compare Page 13 to Page 11.) In earlier Pages, we only had to recognize and identify the differences between the drawing and model. On Page 9, we circled the similarities and on Page 11, the differences. When Pages 12 and 13 are completed, they will look like the earlier Pages because we must draw pictures that are the same as (or different from) the models in the characteristics that are circled.

7. Plan a strategy for working.

8. Teacher's mediation for goal-seeking, goal-planning, and goal-achieving behavior:

Let's do the first task together. What shall we look at first, the example or the words? Let's describe the example verbally and then look at the words. In the model of the first task on Page 12, we see a striped triangle. The circled words are "form" and "size." Can we start to draw? Not yet. Let's look at the model again and check the size. Is that all? No, we must check the other dimensions. "Number" and "color" are not circled so they must be different. We draw one triangle and there is one triangle in the model. How many more triangles shall we draw to make them different in number? Any number we want so long as it is more than one. Aren't there any limits? The size of the frame restricts us because the triangles must be the same size as the one in the model, and we only have a limited amount of room. Now what shall we do about color? We can leave the triangle blank, or color it. We can use any color or pattern we want as long as it isn't striped.

Let's look at the second "picture" frame in the first row. "Number" and "form" are circled. Can we start drawing right away? No, we must first gather all the necessary information, or we will have to erase. The triangle will be different in size and color. Color is added after we draw, so that is all right; but what about the size? It must be different. It can be either larger or smaller than the triangle in the model, but it cannot be the same size. Look at the Page for a moment. What other dimensions must we consider *before* we start to draw? Form and direction. In the frames that have no words circled, we can draw anything we want as long as it is different from the model in all the given attributes. We check our work as we did on Pages 9 and 11, by "reading" the finished picture and the circled words to see if they match: same form, yes; same size, yes; same color, no; same number, no.

9. In task 1, Page 13, the strategy is as follows:

   a. Look at what is given in order to gather all necessary information.

   b. Describe the model (white square in task 1).

   c. Drawing must be different in number, but the same in form (square), size, and color (white).

   d. In the picture 2 frame, the form (square) must differ in size and color from that of the model. The number must be the same.

**All the elements must be processed simultaneously (synchronously) before we start to draw. Otherwise it will be necessary to erase to make each change.**

This is a different way of thinking than in math, chemistry, cooking, and construction. In those subjects we think and work sequentially, one step after another.

10. Similarities are conserved in a variety of areas (e.g., writing a form letter and changing only the name and address of the addressee; using the same knitting pattern and changing the size and color; constructing the same art project, but changing the color and material of construction).

11. Instructions must be read carefully, even if superficially they look the same (e.g., Pages 12 and 13 look the same, their tasks look the same, and the instructions are on the same part of the Page and look almost identical).

*Examples:* Instructions on new appliances; push and pull doors; vending machines; new frying pans that should not be washed with soap.

12. Task 4, second picture frame, Page 13, has all attributes circled. The drawing must be different in everything. The frame cannot be left empty because the instructions say: "Make a drawing."

**In case of doubt as to the procedure, refer back to the instructions.**

13. Differences are conserved in a variety of areas (e.g., the new recording has a different style, intensity, tune, lyrics, but it has the same rock beat; ice cream of a different flavor; mashed potatoes with margarine instead of butter; sweater different in color and size from the one in the store window).

**The stable attributes in these tasks are form or shape, number, and color. The other attributes, size and direction, are relative. Number and color can be made relative by using the dimensions "more" and "less" for number, and "lighter" and "darker" for color or hue. "Size" can become a constant attribute by providing measurements. "Direction" can become constant by using coordinates or compass points.**

# Segment of Lesson
# Page 12

### *Mediation of Regulation and Control of Behavior: Illustrated Behavior*

Teacher: From the example we solved together on the blackboard, we can expect a great deal of difficulty in the exercises on Page 12, can't we? Who would like to remind us what the two main sources of difficulties were? Yes, David.

David: The first difficulty was the need to consider not only what we were told explicitly, but also the data implied by the instructions.

Teacher: Very good, David. And what was the part that was implied by the instructions?

David: That our drawing should not only be the same in the aspects indicated by the circled words but, because of the word "only," it should also be different in the other aspects.

Teacher: Very good. And who could suggest a way that would help us overcome this difficulty? Please, Rebecca.

Rebecca: I think it would be easier for us if we referred to the exercise as having two instructions: 1. The drawing should be the same as the sample in the aspects indicated by the circled words. 2. The drawing should be different from the sample in the aspects indicated by the words that are not circled.

Teacher: Very good, Rebecca. Can we also expect difficulties from another source in these exercises? Yes, Clare.

Clare: We have to remember that we are using the circled words, not the blue words. The color could confuse us.

Teacher: Good observation, Clare. The color of the words is irrelevant. Any other difficulties? Steven.

Steven: We must take into account all the attributes that characterize our drawing simultaneously before we start to draw. Otherwise, we would have to erase and correct several times.

Teacher: Very true, Steven. Can anyone offer a strategy that would help us do this? Yes, Robin.

Robin: What we could do is verbally sum up all the needed attributes and then, following the verbal description, draw the requested picture.

Teacher: Very good, Robin. And now that we've prepared and thought of ways that would help us overcome the difficulties we anticipated, we can go to work. Please do the exercises on the Page.

# Teacher's Guide to Comparisons

# UNIT III

## Objectives

To use induction and deduction to establish classes and class membership.

To find the common attributes of the members of a set.

To discriminate between members and nonmembers of a set.

Pages 14–16

# Analysis in Terms of the Cognitive Map

## Vocabulary

class     set     induction     deduction     justify

## Content

Familiar elements from which to select members of a class.

## Modality

Verbal.

## Phase

### Input

Precise perception of the attributes of an object presented verbally.

Use of several sources of information simultaneously.

Selection of appropriate labels for class members.

### Elaboration

Definition of attributes of a particular category.

Hypothetical thinking and logical evidence as a strategy for selecting members of a set.

Use of product of comparison as a basis for inferences and judgments.

### Output

Delay of response until data have been gathered and elaborated.

## Operations

Identification; generalization; discrimination; categorization.

## Level of abstraction

Moderate in categorization.

## Level of complexity

Low.

## Level of efficiency

Initially low; increases with subsequent Pages.

| Anticipated difficulties due to | Methods of eliminating, bypassing, or overcoming anticipated difficulties |
|---|---|
| Rigidity so that student cannot easily frame new hypothesis and explore it. | Explore with the student the attributes of each of the classes. |
| Impulsivity so that an item that is almost correct is selected. | Discuss class attributes. See if sentence, "Both A and B are members of set X," is appropriate. |

# Suggested Discussion Topics for Insight and/or Bridging

Precise description of an object as a member of an inclusive set (based on similarities) and a subset (based on differences) will aid in its discovery. For example, items in a grocery store and books in the library.

Discussion of where things are categorized for our convenience. For example, zip codes, area codes, departments in a store, species, and countries.

# Page 14

## Objectives

To verbally construct items that differ from one another in given attributes, but that are members of the same superordinate class.

To select items as examples that are simultaneously appropriate to both the description of the common and the different.

## Subgoal

To investigate various divergent responses.

## Vocabulary

| | | | |
|---|---|---|---|
| class | limited | set | family |
| infinite | deduction | criteria | |

## Mediation

Mediation of a feeling of competence and of individuation and psychological differentiation is elicited by tasks that require selection from among many alternative responses. Mediation of meaning is indicated as this and later Pages prepare for categorization.

# Page 14 (AV 6)

**14**

In each of the following exercises, you are given the similarity and differences. Fill in what is missing so that your answers are described by the given information.

| | citrus fruits | yellow |
| | | orange |

| | paper products | for reading |
| | | for writing |

| | in the classroom | studies |
| | | teaches |

| | vehicles | on water |
| | | in the air |

| | numbers | a multiple of 3 |
| | | not a multiple of 3 |

| | cities in North America | on the West Coast |
| | | on the East Coast |

© 1995 R. Feuerstein, HWCRI, Jerusalem. Comparisons

SkyLight
PROFESSIONAL DEVELOPMENT

© 1995 by R. Feuerstein, Hadassah–Wizo–Canada Research Institute.

# Introduction and Discussion

1. After decoding the instructions, decide on a strategy.

2. Decide on starting point (refer to Organization of Dots).

    a. We read from left to right. We wash a floor from the back of the room to the door. We write on paper from top to bottom.

    b. In these tasks, we must start with the middle column.

3. The middle column contains the name of each "family." It designates the kinds of things that are related to each other. It is based on what is common. If we look at what is in common first, we know to which "family," or set, the two words we are seeking belong. It is efficient because the family is limited in its members, and it narrows our field of search (e.g., we look in an atlas for maps and in a dictionary for the meaning of words).

4. We are not interested in just any example of things that are orange and yellow, but in citrus fruits that are those colors.

---

**To solve the problem, we use the deductive process. We move from the generalization to specific examples. To check our work, we use the inductive process. We move from the examples to the class.**

---

5. We must move from the set (family) to attributes that describe the difference before choosing the appropriate items.

6. Tasks differ in the number of possible answers.

    a. Some tasks have only a limited number of answers (e.g., a classroom usually has only one teacher and many students).

    b. Some tasks require choosing from among a few answers (e.g., orange citrus fruit = orange, tangerine, kumquat; yellow citrus fruit = grapefruit, lemon, pomelo).

    c. Some tasks will have many answers, all of which match the criteria (e.g., the number of cities on the east and west coast of North America).

d. Some tasks will have infinite possibilities (e.g., numbers divisible by 3).

**From the time we get up in the morning to the time we go to sleep, we constantly select items from sets to match our needs.**

*Examples:* eating breakfast, going to work or school, attending classes, etc.

# Pages 15–16

*Note:* Pages 15 and 16 are taught together.

## Objectives

To select items that are appropriate simultaneously to the description of the set and the subsets.

To show an increased flexibility in choosing parameters for comparison and examples of their application.

To demonstrate mastery of the process of comparison.

## Vocabulary

format        mastery

## Mediation

Mediation of a feeling of competence is elicited in the interpretation of tasks that introduce sets, principles of classification, and set members. The variety of possible responses require mediation of individuation and psychological differentiation.

## Page 15

Name two things that have the common property listed and are different from each other in the way specified. Be sure that you have chosen correctly.

| | Common | Different | Words |
|---|---|---|---|
| Example | furniture | its use | chair<br>cupboard |
| 1 | clothes | season | |
| 2 | tools | their use | |
| 3 | cities | their country | |
| 4 | vehicles | their speed | |

## Page 16

Name two things that have the common property listed and are different from each other in the way specified. Be sure that you have chosen correctly.

| | Common | Different | Words |
|---|---|---|---|
| 5 | geographical features | their height | |
| 6 | buildings | their occupants | |
| 7 | buildings | their size | |
| 8 | mail | its weight | |
| 9 | lights | their strength | |

## Introduction and Discussion

*Note:* Discussion may follow independent work. Independent work can be evaluated to indicate mastery.

1. Compare these tasks to those in previous Pages.

    a. Similar in format to Page 14.

    b. Similar in need to simultaneously identify similarities and differences between objects as in Pages 9, 11, 12, and 13.

    c. Similar in need to construct as in Pages 12 and 13. Differ from those Pages in modality. These Pages are verbal.

2. Instructions limit us to a set (family) and subsets based on a given parameter.

3. Many correct divergent responses are possible because of the great number of items that are members of the set and meet the criteria.

4. The members of a set can be described or classified according to many different attributes. In task 6, Page 16, the occupants of the buildings need not necessarily be human.

    *Examples:* Flowers can be classified according to color, size, kind, freshness, blooming season, self-seeding ability, sun or shade requirements, etc. Students can be classified according to gender, grade, age, vocational subject, major subject, future occupation, extracurricular activities, etc.

5. Flexibility in thought is required to discover all the parameters and apply them.

---

**In these Pages, we will summarize what we have learned about sets, or families. In our next instrument, Categorization, we will classify items into sets (groups, families) and break down the sets into their parts.**

# ADDITIONAL
# Instrumental Enrichment Resources

### THE MAKING OF THE INDIVIDUAL
**LEARNING HOW TO LEARN**
*An Interview with Reuven Feuerstein*
Produced by James Bellanca
30-minute videotape   $99.95....**#1224**
Feuerstein discusses how to prepare students for the twenty-first century by helping them learn how to learn, teaching with high expectations, and building thinking skills through mediated learning.

### MAKING STUDENTS SMARTER
**FROM THEORY TO PRACTICE**
Reuven Feuerstein
Two 60-minute audio-
tapes   $29.95....**#1227**
Psychologist Reuven Feuerstein, the creator of Instrumental Enrichment, discusses his theories of structural cognitive modifiability and mediated learning. Feuerstein believes all students, including the culturally disadvantaged, disabled, and underachieving gifted, can expand their intelligence. Learn the premise behind the theories and how they work.

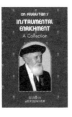

### ON FEUERSTEIN'S INSTRUMENTAL ENRICHMENT
**A COLLECTION**
Edited by Meir Ben-Hur
288 pages/paper   $21.95....**#1256**
This collection offers readers a comprehensive look at the most recent writings about Instrumental Enrichment. The collection comprises three sections—the first explains Feuerstein's theory of cognitive modifiability, the second examines the latest research findings, and the third discusses the application of this methodology.

### CHANGING CHILDREN'S MINDS
**FEUERSTEIN'S REVOLUTION IN THE TEACHING OF INTELLIGENCE**
Howard Sharron
381 pages/paper   $32.00....**#1290**
This insightful book explores Feuerstein's theory that all children can learn. Learn how Instrumental Enrichment can empower underachieving students through the dynamic notion of intellectual potential.

### THE MIND OF A CHILD
Videotape   $40.00....**#1419**
A one-hour documentary that follows two extraordinary teachers and their work with aboriginal children in British Columbia and students in inner-city Washington, D.C. The film documents the breakthroughs these teachers experienced in adapting Reuven Feuerstein's theory of Instrumental Enrichment to their students.

### WHAT IS IT ABOUT ME YOU CAN'T TEACH?
*An Instructional Guide for the Urban Educator*
Eleanor Reneé Rodriguez & James Bellanca
192 pages/paper   $30.95....**#1444**
Beginning with Reuven Feuerstein's pioneering work, the authors of this valuable resource identify hundreds of practical classroom methods to help educators determine the best means for putting "high expectation" theory into practice in urban schools.

### MEDIATED LEARNING IN AND OUT OF THE CLASSROOM
Manual Work Team of the Cognitive Research Program
208 pages/paper   $30.95....**#1446**
This layperson's guide shows parents, teachers, and counselors how to implement professor Feuerstein's theory of mediated learning to enhance all children's learning potential. Mediated learning can improve students' impulse control, ability to make accurate comparisons, orientation in time and space, understanding of cause and effect, and other higher-order thinking processes.

### TO ORDER THESE ITEMS, CALL
# 800-348-4474

2626 S. Clearbrook Dr., Arlington Heights, IL 60005
800-348-4474 • 847-290-6600 • (FAX) 847-290-6609